handiwork

Also by Sara Baume

Spill Simmer Falter Wither
A Line Made by Walking

handiwork

SARA BAUME

TRAMPPRESS

First published in 2020 by Tramp Press
www.tramppress.com

A CIP record for this title is
available from the British library.

1 3 5 7 9 10 8 6 4 2

Paperback ISBN 978-1-9164342-5-7
Ebook ISBN 978-1-9164342-8-8

Tramp Press gratefully acknowledges the
financial assistance of the Arts Council.

Thank you for supporting independent publishing.

Set in 12 pt on 15.5 pt Fournier by Marsha Swan.
Printed by Clays, London.

for Dad

'AMATEURS', STEPHEN KNOTT writes in *Amateur Craft: History and Theory*, 'have their own convoluted, inefficient and superfluous processes of production that reflect their subjectivity and freedom from the obligation to produce a defined output.'

THERE IS AN ALASKAN SONGBIRD, the northern wheatear. She weighs about as much as a small ball of wool, and every autumn she flies about as far as 300,000 balls of wool unspooled in a westerly direction, disentangled across Siberia and Kazakhstan and Iraq and Saudi Arabia, finally coming to a definitive stop in East Africa. It takes her three months to get there and two-and-a-half months to get back again, and so the northern wheatear devotes almost half of every year to these journeys which she makes out of countless individual flaps – beating her wings continuously against winds prevailing and preternatural over the course of 30,000 kilometres of sky.

There are easier routes she could take; there are places with clement climates far closer to Alaska than sub-Saharan Africa, but the northern wheatear doesn't choose them; she doesn't choose at all.

Every autumn, she follows the route her ancestors initiated at the end of the last Ice Age, 10,000 years ago – the convoluted, inefficient, superfluous directions that are her genetic inheritance.

And then, in spring, she goes the same way back again.

I HEAR THE STORY of the northern wheatear on a day in spring, from a podcast which I listen to sitting in the straight-backed chair at the eastern end of the living room table. I sit there every day between the hours of twelve and four, parallel to the windowsill and overshadowed by a row of books, a Christmas cactus, and a dusty globe which encapsulates a long-expired lightbulb. When I retell a version of the story of the journey of the northern wheatear to Mark, later in the evening – a slightly erroneous, airily embellished version – he remarks that there are fish who swim against the current – salmon and herring who live in the open sea but are compelled to travel back to the rivers and streams in which they were born in order to spawn – and this gives me cause to remember a tiny goldfish I owned for a year or so in my early twenties who, on the occasion of having her water changed, would make every effort to resist being poured from a corner of her narrow tank into a giant mayonnaise jar.

The goldfish would go to the place where the last of the water pooled as the glass was lifted. She would turn her face to point in the opposite direction of the tilt. She would push against the force of gravity and the flow of water, wriggling her entire body, as if burrowing upwards through thick soil.

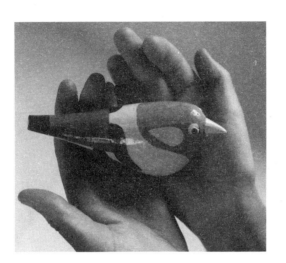

'THE WORKSHOP IS the craftsman's home,' Richard Sennett writes in *The Craftsman*. 'Traditionally this was literally so. In the Middle Ages craftsmen slept, ate, and raised their children in the places where they worked.'

THIS HOUSE is a house of industry.

It has four bedrooms, only one of which is devoted to sleep.

THE STRAIGHT-BACKED CHAIR at the eastern end of the living room table, parallel to the windowsill and its clutter, is one of several workstations dispersed between rooms, starting outside the back door with the rusted yard tap and extending all the way through to the weatherworn garden bench.

THE SHORT STRETCH OF countertop alongside the kitchen sink is a mixing station. There's a sack of modelling plaster and a stack of plastic containers rescued from the recycling bin – the tall, round pots of yoghurt and the flimsy trays of rectangular biscuits – fig rolls, malted milks, custard creams. There's a porcelain scoop for measuring the correct ratio of plaster to water, and a tall-stemmed teaspoon for whisking the powdery lumps away. Wet plaster must be creamy. Once poured, I bump the base of the mould gently against the surface of the countertop in order to hustle any residual air to the surface, to set it free. Tiny bubbles obligingly rise and burst – a stippled pattern of negative space appears.

A SIGNIFICANT PATCH of floor in front of the unused hearth in what would have traditionally been the 'good front room' and which is now the guest bedroom is a sawing station. A miniature scroll saw trails from a socket and sits on a mat of shaped foam. Adjacent to the saw's table, there's just enough space for me to kneel before it as I work – a person-sized circle cleared in the sand-coloured dust. Behind the clearing and the saw, there's a box of cuts and offcuts – balsa and ply, pine dowels and cherrywood lathes. Strewn about the lino and the rag-rugs, there's sandpaper of varying grits – from course to fine and from unfolded to extensively folded.

THE LOW COFFEE TABLE in front of the sofa, which faces the log stove and the TV set, is a painting station. A glass jar of brushes is permanently accompanied by another of cloudy water, and a ball of clotted kitchen roll. The ferrules of the brushes are narrow and wide, rounded and straight; the bristles are natural and synthetic, soft and rough, filbert and fanned. I only ever use the same three, the plainest three, but I keep them all because I am constantly susceptible to future projects – to the possibility that some day I might be confronted with a surface that requires a more exotic class of stroke. Beneath the table, on top of a large tub of white emulsion, there's a dish of contorted tubes of acrylic paint and a thickly blotched palette in a ziplock bag.

THIS IS THE STATION where each evening comes to an end. I spend its final three hours cross-legged on the sofa; the same cushion I use as a tray to eat my dinner off becomes a platform upon which to apply paint to a succession of small objects after dinner has been eaten. The television flickers and I listen to it. In most cases, a story can be followed from sound alone, but I glance up every now and again in order to identify speakers, in order to maintain some kind of visual momentum through each programme. At dinnertime, a drinking vessel is added to the other glasses on the low coffee table and so it often happens, as the evening wears on, that I plop a sullied brush into the clear water, or take a thoughtless sip of the paint-tainted stuff.

AS EACH WORKING DAY ends on the sofa, it starts upstairs on the swivelling office chair in front of my writing desk. During the course of an ordinary day, between the swivel chair and the sofa cushions, I shift from station to station according to the hour's demands, returning most predictably to the eastern end of the table in the living room.

There, in the nook beneath the windowsill, I keep a narrow timber box of knives. Inside, there are several handles and an assortment of steel blades – flat, pointed, curved, tapered, some sharp and some blunt but most at some stop along the trajectory of decline from mint to spent, unused to overused.

It is important to differentiate between sharpnesses. The sharpness of each blade dictates the pressure applied by my carving hand, the speed and ease at which each shuck of set plaster slips away from its block and into crumb. Between the surface of the table and the knife box and the plaster blocks and the crumb pile, there's a sheath of old newspapers positioned to protect the table-top, even though there's already a jagged tear in the cotton and a tracery of stab marks in the vinyl.

Somehow I never manage to remember to place down a protective layer until after some initial damage has been done.

THE LIVING-ROOM table station attracts the paraphernalia of other practices. There's a pile of sketchbooks and a carton of colouring pencils, several post-its glued to the window frame – they are luminous pink, green and yellow; they are measurements and calculations, instructions and reminders; they are mantras, spells, codes. Underneath the table, resting against the wall, there's a long stick half-coated in thick paint – this is the implement I use to stir the huge tub of emulsion and its resting end has left a row of faint crescents in its wake – a pattern of new brilliant white on old brilliant white, which only becomes visible on fine evenings when a rectangle of sun from the opposing window does a searchlight circuit of the room and touches that particular strip of wall.

WHEN WE FIRST MOVED into this house, I assigned myself a room where I would write. I carried in a desk and tucked the swivel chair beneath it and raised a bastion of books around it. As for the other stations, they have never been formally designated. Instead, they have asserted themselves gradually, as if the walls and floors and furniture are somehow sympathetic to my preoccupations and repetitions and observances; as if this house has diligently ordered itself around my daily practices, my daily handiwork.

THE TRAIN STATION of a small city in western Germany, summer, a dozen years ago.

The silhouette of my head and shoulders as it creeps across the miniature landscape of a model railway contained within the walls and ceiling of an ample glass box.

REMEMBERING THIS SCENE, I struggle to picture the train – the sole element which ought to have been moving. Instead, I remember every unmoving element: footpaths, roads and rail tracks climbing, cutting and snaking through fields, villages and forests, and then the densely spaced, meticulously ordered props: buildings, trees, telegraph poles, livestock, people, even birds – each glued to a single spot, stalled in a single moment – interrupted, petrified.

'THE MINIATURE, linked to nostalgic versions of childhood and history', Susan Stewart writes in *On Longing: Narratives of the Miniature, the Gigantic, the Souvenir, the Collection*, 'presents a diminutive, and thereby maniputable, version of experience, a version which is domesticated and protected from contamination.'

THAT WAS THE SUMMER I graduated from art college and then flew to Italy for several weeks of volunteer work with the Venice Biennale, followed by a roundabout journey home again – a migration northwards – overland by bus and train with pauses, in no particular order, for documenta 12 in Kassel, the decennial Skulptur Projekte in Münster, the Pinakothek der Moderne in Munich, the Kunst-Werke Institute in Berlin, the Kunsthalle Bern, the Kunstmuseum Basel, and the Stedelijk Museum Amsterdam – experiencing works of every medium and dimension – from marble and cement to sound and light, from the monumental to the ephemeral – by artists from almost every country of the world, alive and dead.

I REMEMBER: a top bunk in a communal tent, an itchy felt blanket, a dark rye roll embedded with apricots, a fountain with staggeringly tall spouts and the sun catching every droplet. I remember the grimy cord of a window blind in a hostel dormitory, a train that went nowhere for a whole night in order that its passengers might attempt a full sleep, a spliff I was too afraid to join in the smoking of – too afraid of the likely loss of control – and all the slightly different vending machines with their slightly different merchandise.

I remember: awe, fascination, revelation, a disorienting eruption of newness, and yet, by the time the trip was almost over, in August in the train station of a small city in western Germany, I was still capable of being charmed by the model railway.

The persistent memory that defines that summer is the shadow of my standing self cast across the static landscape – a cloud passing over a miniature universe, a perfect universe – protected from contamination.

THE MODEL PROPS and scenery were composed of plaster, plastic, soft woods, fine felts and strong glues. The colours were bleeding shades of yellow, red, green and brown. Apart from a glassy little duck pond, the scenery inside the cabinet bore only negligible traces of blue.

There is, I realised, no sky in a model railway. In the hobby shop, on the rack that displays the landscaping materials, amongst the packets of seafoam trees and miscellaneous hedging, tarmac and ballast scatters, grass flocks and rolls of spring green mats and summer and autumn and winter green mats, there has never been, on the market right up until this present moment, a fabric available for the replication of firmament.

The model railway's sky is the same as the real one – both there and not, ungraspable yet ubiquitous.

WITHOUT SKY, the model birds in model railways tend not to seem as if they are flying – plastic doves are glued to plastic rocks, mallards to the glassy varnish of round ponds and straight canals. Pigeons, crows and gulls – the omnipresent species – perch on power lines and roof ridges. Only the predatory birds – buzzards, falcons, harriers, hawks – are occasionally skewered onto short, slim sticks, their wings outstretched in postures of flight.

AT THE VERY BEGINNING of the autumn that came after the very end of the summer of my Grand European Tour, I moved home to my parents' house – my place of birth and point of origin, my nesting grounds – and signed on for the dole.

In the wardrobe of my old bedroom, at intervals along the timber shelves, in every drawer and under the bed, I was greeted by the objects I had made as a child: the models and trinkets and figurines I had once re-conceptualised from actual scenes, machines and creatures, and pieced together out of the available fragments of my material environment – a practice that Charles Jencks in the early 1970s designated *adhocism*: 'a method of creation relying particularly on resources which are already at hand' – although, of course, I wouldn't have known this at the time.

A fimo elephant, a tinfoil spaceship, several painted pebbles and cereal-box skyscrapers, a pair of polystyrene robins.

THAT SUMMER, MY DAD — who had never wholly understood the concept-driven, studiously ironic assemblages of found materials I produced in college, who would wonder as he trailed around end-of-term exhibitions behind my mum why I spent so much time working so obsessively to make only just these useless, pretty things — converted his old greenhouse into a makeshift studio. He furnished it with a wall of deep shelves, a sliding glass door and a sturdy work bench, so that when his travelling daughter returned home in August, it would be to an unobstructed space where she could get straight down to work on the strange art he did not understand.

KNITTED FISH, pressed flowers, baskets of glued-down shells, paper boats, paper planes, paper hats, dead twigs collaged with paper leaves – small objects I had once put to use as decoration, gifts, games – small objects I had never questioned the meaning of or attempted to invent meaning for; small objects which, laid down side by side across an open space, would no doubt add up to a substantial trail – a material testimonial of eighteen years of curiosity and investigation.

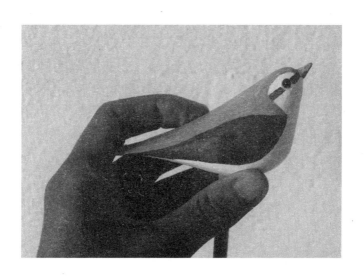

THIS HOUSE OF INDUSTRY has, conversely, the potential to be magnificently silent – when the radio isn't playing, or a podcast; when there aren't any cows in the facing field; when the wind drops, and the rain stops.

PEOPLE ARE USUALLY SURPRISED when I tell them that I listen to talk radio as I write. I must then try to explain how I find magnificent silence to be almost aggressive, how the near-noiselessness of writing is, for me, intimidating enough in itself. The cursor makes no sound as it weaves around the screen of the laptop; the tip of my index finger circling the touch-pad is a whisper; the tap of a struck key scarcely louder, and then there are the hesitations. Most of the time, I play the radio so quietly that I can't decipher what the topic is anyway – I play it solely for the comradeship of a soft, sputtering stream of voice. At more onerous times I allow myself a little extra volume – a topic of interest is an indulgence, a moment of release from the suspense of thinking. I hover over my inbox with the same intention. An indulgence makes it easier to continue, momentarily dispelling the preciousness of the thing that I am doing and the duress to do it with exactitude.

THERE ARE NO SONGBIRDS here, in the hinterland of this house of industry or, at least, none that linger.

WHEN WE FIRST ARRIVED, there was a busted feeder beside the concrete garden wall beneath the sycamore, and Mark, who is taller, hung up an identical but intact one on the lowest, thickest branch, and it lasted only a day or two before a rampant south-westerly blew it down. For the first couple of weeks we shifted the feeder about between different points of the washing line and the tree, until the wind dislodged it for the final time and it cracked, like its predecessor, against the wall.

The feeder had travelled with us from our former garden where it had dangled from a nail in the cement of the back of the house for five years, attracting no attention from other than a passing chaffinch, and since then I have convinced myself that songbirds will only successfully establish in gardens they recognise from collective memory – gardens their ancestors frequented in generations past.

Instead of the chirrup of feeding songbirds, ours is the cackle of far-off gulls.

AFTER NOON, I am less in need of the comradeship of strangers' voices. In contrast to the near-silence of the practice of writing, handiwork requires constant movement and generates its own soft, sputtering racket, like a summons, I sometimes think — like incantations of the meeting of material and tool.

IT IS IMPORTANT to listen, so the birders say, as important as it is to watch – or even more – because often you will only know which direction to turn your head from the sound of the song.

THE SOUND of the mixing station is the muffled tinkling of a teaspoon, and then the soft bump-bump-bump of plastic packaging against laminated countertop.

The sound of the carving station is the stabbing and scraping of sharp steel against moist plaster.

The sound of the painting station is the dabbing of a blunted brush against thrice-primed china.

The sound of the sawing station is the puttering of a diminutive motor, and then the rasping of light wood against the teeth of a slender blade.

Often I sit outside on the garden bench in order to sand, and this sound – in summer inescapably accompanied by gull-cackle and insect-hum – is the shush-shush-shushing obliteration of the finest splinters and final anomalies.

THE SOUND MARK MAKES is a thump or rattle or scuff or step, the tap as it runs, the kettle as it boils, the mew and click of a door. At intervals, as we drift between stations, we pause to speak to one another, not really saying anything of consequence but making simple flight calls – like geese gently honking to the fellow members of their formation as they flap – reassuring the others that they are still nearby and still, to some extent, on course.

EVERY GOOSE I HAVE SEEN in my life has been in a city – on the banks of squalid ponds, jabbing at the surface of soggy football pitches.

They tend to travel in family flocks, but many other birds forge groups along less exclusive lines in preparation for migration – fashioning new families in accordance with their changing circumstances, their changing selves. Sometimes several different species will come together, providing they occupy the same position on the food chain and share a general destination, but there are also birds who migrate alone, such as the tiny willow warbler.

AT TEN GRAMS and twelve centimetres, in her inaugural year of life, she departs all by herself and in the dark. In summer, in excess of two million willow warblers from central and southern Africa flock into our treetops and meet again – singling one another out between the twitching leaves. She has a yellowish supercilium but is otherwise pale brownish-green. She is inconspicuous – her terrific forbearance concealed beneath her foliage-coloured plumage.

As she flies, her body clock adjusts in line with the earth's axis. Without experience, without guidance, without visibility – the tiny willow warbler always knows what time it is.

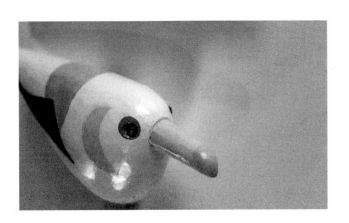

I HAVE ALWAYS FELT caught between two languages, though I can only speak in one.

The one I can speak goes down on paper and into my laptop, in the hours before noon. The one I cannot speak goes down in small painted objects, in the hours after.

The more I need to explain, the longer the documents become, the larger the assemblages.

I HAVE ALWAYS FELT a terrible responsibility for time.

I WORRY THAT THE THING I am doing at any given moment may not be the best possible thing for that particular moment. Should I be reading, writing, carving, painting, I ask myself – and then even after the decision has been made – is this the book I should be reading; the sentence I should be writing; the form I should be carving; the carved object I should be painting?

THOUGH THERE IS no such thing as time devoid of obligation, there are periods of each day that I am forced to set aside from work: pendulous phases devoted to nothing greater than the general preservation of my body and perpetuation of its functions.

From sleep to sleep, an awful lot of time is suspended in this way, maybe even most of it. The time I spend un-balling my socks in the morning, brushing my teeth, lifting mugs and bowls and plates out of cupboards and drawers and off hooks, chopping and frying and tossing vegetables, sending emails, washing my hands, putting mugs and bowls and plates back into cupboards and drawers and onto hooks, replying to emails, balling my socks up again at night.

Even when I am spending time with family, walking my dogs, swimming in the sea, drinking with friends; even when I am enjoying time – especially when I am enjoying time – I perceive my real life to have stalled.

Every hour, every minute, every second spent absent from a workstation is a class of flapping on the spot, of keeping in the air, but failing to propel forward.

Every day is a day-long crusade to correct this imbalance between productivity and drudgery, stimulation and stagnation – crusades further complicated by the tendency phases have to bleed, for there are different states of making as there are different stages of migration. There is an amorphous period of accession, and then later, a similarly amorphous period of retreat.

There is the building up of fat reserves, the necessary stopovers, the orientation and reorientation.

Most of the time spent making is spent, in fact, in the approach.

BETWEEN THE ACCESSIONS and retreats, the take-offs and descents, come rare phases of flow, of soaring.

STEPHEN KNOTT DEFINES the concept of *flow* as 'utopia in a moment: an atemporal release and liberation from capitalist time and its schedules by intense concentration on an activity'.

IN THE STATE OF FLOW, I am concentrating solely upon the microcosm of my eyes and hands, the tools and materials and burgeoning object on the table in front of me. I am making a sequence of small decisions almost unconsciously – how hard to assert the pressure of the carving knife; how many more strokes to apply, in what direction, and where. Flow is a continuous assessment of the object within reach – the size and shape and symmetry of each separate part, the facility with which they fit with one another, the whole.

For a brief, brilliant moment at the peak of flow, my thoughts will reach no further than the limits of my object and time passes faster because I forget to check what time it is.

Flow is a forgetting – to press the slim button on the side of my phone which illuminates the screen; a forgetting to plan what I'm preparing for lunch; a forgetting to check and see what the dog is barking at; a forgetting to piss even though my bladder is uncomfortably full.

FLOW IS A TAILWIND.

And the bird with the most expansive wingspan – the wandering albatross – is able, in favourable conditions, to soar for vast distances expending the bare minimum of energy.

On a single strong beat of her tremendous wings – together the length of a transit van, the mast of a sailboat, a telegraph pole – the wandering albatross glides across the Southern Ocean.

THE TAILWIND BECOMES a headwind around about the point where rationalisation begins. John Ruskin is said to have observed that with the security of knowing how to do something with reasonable skill 'comes a great boredom'. And in spite of all of the suspended time I spend longing for and striving toward one or another of my workstations, the approaches are tedious, sometimes sickeningly so.

Every day, I complete a single carved plaster object, and every day each completed object comes to precisely the breadth of the limits of my patience.

I MUST STOP ONCE the boredom becomes intolerable, knowing that if I plunge on past this point I will risk arriving at resentment, and this will fundamentally contaminate the genuineness of the thing — because sour feelings make a soured object, and people will be able to recognise this, and even if they don't —

I will be able to recognise it.

I HAVE ALWAYS FELT a terrible responsibility for time.

This impotent urgency manifests at minimum as an internalised twitch, at maximum as the murmuring of a voice inside my head, arguing that the solid form at hand is not symmetrical enough – the wrong angle, the wrong shape, the wrong stroke – causing me to carve it smaller and smaller in the name of an inconceivable perfection – to carve it away completely, back into plaster dust.

The nemesis voice never acquiesces to flow; it is always reasoning and glancing ahead into the coming weather. *You could stop now*, the voice murmurs, *or you could get ahead for tomorrow*. And then, tomorrow – *you could stop now*, it will murmur, *or you could get ahead for tomorrow* …

Like the migrant birds who, one year, find they have to go a little farther than the year before – for a superior food source, a safer resting spot, because the weather is peculiar.

And then, again, the year after, a little farther still –

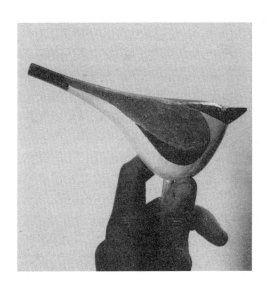

IT SEEMS TO ME, increasingly, that it might be possible to make up poetic facts about bird migration – that buntings, for example, learn how to read the stars; that pintails carry tiny magnets in their beaks; that the chances of recovering the ankle-ring of a ruby-throated hummingbird is one in a thousand – that would later turn out to be true.

THE FIRST RECORDED INSTANCE of bird banding occurred in Pennsylvania in the early years of the nineteenth century. A French *émigré* called John James Audubon noticed a pair of eastern phoebes – a songbird native to North and South America – nesting in a cave on his father's estate. Curious as to whether or not it was the same family of phoebes who came back every spring, he removed two chicks from the nest and tied a silver thread around their ankles, loosely yet securely, and the following year the grown birds in their ankle bracelets returned to the cave to nest, and Audubon was thrilled and gratified and captivated.

THE EASTERN PHOEBE has an onomatopoeic name; she calls *fee-bee, fee-bee* just at the cuckoo calls *cuck-oo* and the curlew calls *cour-looouu* and the chiffchaff calls *chiff-chiff-chiff-chaff-chiff-chaff-chiff-chiff* – only they don't, or they do depending upon the way you hear it, or the way you arrange sounds into letters of the alphabet in your mind, or whether or not you knew the bird's name before hearing it in the first place.

I THINK OF MY DAD when I hear the story of Audubon
– of a man who wore hard-wearing clothes always, who
harboured an opaque obsession with an unattainable task –
my dad in his steel-toed boots and grease-scented overalls,
with a coat of dust further greying his thinning hair.

My dad, who demolished a greenhouse to build me a studio.

My dad, who, every spring, witnessed the reappearance of
a family of migrant birds.

FOR THE LAST THIRTY-TWO YEARS of his life and the first thirty-two of mine, my dad worked in a sandstone quarry surrounded by countryside. For over three decades, he spent every weekday alone in the lunar landscape, operating and maintaining the heavy machinery, much of which he had rebuilt or helped to build or built himself completely. He was a master of what Stephen Knott describes as the 'scratch-built' – things that have been 'entirely constructed by hand' as opposed to merely assembled out of readymade components. Whereas Knott used the term in the context of railway modelling, my dad was a scratch-builder of the monumental – his most tremendous construction was a thirty-tonne rock crusher almost 300 feet long.

EVERY SPRING, from the vantage of his cabin in the tremendous crusher, my dad would watch for the return of a fistful of dainty songbirds.

The sandstone quarry was a monstrous, ravaged, hostile environment for humans – but for the quarry swallows, it was a sanctuary. Unbothered by the noise and dust and desolation, they chose it as a place to nest, year in year out, for the cracks and nooks and shelter provided by iron, steel and rock.

FROM MY DAD, I inherited a propensity for handiwork, but also the terrible responsibility, the killing insistence.

He would leave for the quarry every morning at half-past seven and even after returning from work in the evening he would go out to his shed or his garden, depending upon the season, and remain there until nine at night, hewing away, generating the sound of bashing, clanging, whirring and grinding, as well as an occasional shower of sparks or a sudden blinding flash. On Sunday afternoons, he would sit uneasily amongst us – his rough-skinned, muscular hands flopped to his lap, twitching.

His hands were permanently calloused and oil-stained; he held even his knife and fork as if they were tools.

IN *LIVING ON THE WIND: Across the Hemisphere with Migratory Birds* Scott Weidensaul explains the term *ʒugunruhe* as 'the nocturnal restlessness that European birdkeepers noticed centuries ago in their caged nightingales and other captive songbirds. In spring and fall, the birds began fluttering in their cages just before sunset, continuing until a few hours after midnight – the same period, it turns out, as the peak of nocturnal migration each night.'

Farmed salmon, Mark tells me, show signs of *ʒugunruhe* too – jumping vainly into the air above their net-roofed pens.

EVERYTHING MY DAD made with his twitching hands was unlovely yet practical, and there was a time when I would wonder what he spent so much time working so ferociously for, if not for acclaim. There was a time when I couldn't imagine how anyone might be so obsessed with the realisation of objects that were not beautiful, that were not art.

But my dad just needed to be doing things, to be useful, to be busy – labour was his pleasure, or perhaps his sanctuary.

AFTER HE DIED, my mum took photographs of all of the things he had scratch-built around the house and garden and inside his sheds – machinery, furniture, gates, paths, customised polytunnels and greenhouses, as well as dozens of items that were unclassifiable. They were old and new, rusted and freshly painted, broken and fixed and refixed – they were made from parts of things he had made previously, and sundered and remade. My mum collaged the photographs inside a large frame and gifted it to me – a strange portrait of my dead dad's material testimonial – what Susan Stewart would call 'a compendium which is an autobiography'.

See what he made, my mum was trying to say. See the things and places in which he still lives.

MY DAD, WHO NEVER READ the novel I wrote, but as soon as it was published – as soon as it had been embodied between covers; as soon as it took up a small portion of physical space in the world – came to an understanding that I had achieved something.

THE SWALLOWS WHO STILL ARRIVE every spring in the quarry where my dad used to work leave no perceptible trace of their journey – no swallow contrails across a clear sky – other than on their own, spare bodies. In some cases a long migration can take a barbaric toll on a bird's anatomy, such that she sheds half of her body weight; such that her muscle tissue wastes and her liver shrivels; such that her intestines commence to digest themselves.

I HAVE MY DAD'S HANDS – the length of his fingers, the width of his knuckle-bones – and as I age I watch them grow to resemble his in condition as well – rough-skinned and muscular, calloused and stained. 'Physical prehension is lopsided,' Richard Sennett writes. 'We reach for things with one hand more than the other – in most humans, with the right hand.'

I am like most humans reaching for things – it's my right side that bears the brunt of my handiwork; my right hand that is permanently scabbed by super-glue and impaled with splinters. It's also my right hand that is most exposed to the cold air of the house in winter, and because I lack the patience to wait for warm water to come through the tap, or the good sense not to grip a hot mug or press my palm against the glowing door of the log stove, it's my right fingers that undergo the annual cycle of chilblains – beginning with the first frosts of November, the joints swelling and the skin reddening and blistering, then the joints contracting and the skin fissuring, only for the cycle to begin again, to continue sometimes right the way through to summer.

A FRIEND GIFTS ME hand cream, in a tin with a beautiful Chinese woman wearing a *cheongsam* on the lid, holding a pink orchid against her chest like a sword. I love the tin as an object, but I don't see the point in applying the cream. Tonight I will apply cream and sleep with soft hands, but tomorrow I will set my hands back to work and only need to apply cream again by night.

And so I have decided to save myself this ten seconds of dead time at least.

THERE IS A CHILBLAIN SENSATION – not pain so much as stiffness and itching. There is a faint cramping – it rises from the claw formed by my right fist in order to clasp the carving knife and it abates after a few days of consistent practice – the muscles adjusting – but it returns if I neglect to practise consistently – the muscles forgetting. There is an aching sensation – it runs from my right wrist up to my right shoulder and, after approximately twenty minutes of vigorous sanding, always intensifies to the point at which I am forced to switch activity.

I DON'T UNDERSTAND WHY my whole right side isn't drastically brawny in comparison to my left – why I haven't developed the grotesque physique of a professional arm wrestler. Some silent process of the body decides how to counterbalance my preoccupations, in the same way as it decides to toughen certain fingertips, in the same way it decides whether to reject or assimilate each individual splinter – in the same way that the silent processes of a starling's body understand that she must annually moult but that she cannot lose too many of her flight feathers simultaneously, and so she moults incrementally over the course of several weeks, one feather at a time.

My body knows better than me; it compensates.

THE SICKLES OF DRIED PAINT I never have the patience to fully scrub from the clefts of my fingernails mirror the row of brilliant white crescents along the living room wall – as if I am the house, or the house is me.

I AM NOT COMPLETELY unsympathetic toward my body's silent processes – there are token gestures I make to help keep certain crucial organs from harm; there are costumes of protection.

On behalf of my lungs, a dinted dust mask dangles by its baggy elastic from a panel pin above the mixing station.

On behalf of my eyes, a pair of grazed safety glasses are slung over the carriage of the scroll saw.

MARK TELLS ME about cannibalism in fish; this is one of the reasons why certain species choose a convoluted route of migration. Herring, he says, are unable to identify their own offspring – to recognise a fully-formed fish from a single blob in the jellied mass of discharged roe – and so they must travel a triangular loop between their respective grounds for spawning, feeding and nursing in order to avoid meeting, and accidentally eating, their estranged children.

Mark says he heard a story on the radio about how the tentacles of cephalopods – octopuses, squid and cuttlefish – each think and decide independently of the others, and of the cephalopod as a whole.

IN THE CUPBOARD under the kitchen sink, there's an unopened box of disposable latex gloves.

I have never perforated its seal; never pulled on and peeled off a single pair of its contents.

'INDEED, VERY FEW PEOPLE are aware', José Saramago writes in *The Cave*, 'that in each of our fingers, located somewhere between the first phalange, the mesophalange and the metaphalange, there is a tiny brain.'

BIRD RINGERS ARE AWARE: they refuse to wear gloves during the ringing process. It is important, they say, to feel the heft of a bird in the hand, to know it as a physical presence; the texture of plumage against skin, the fidget of wing against palm; even when it is an apoplectic blue tit, fresh from the dark of the cloth bag, repeatedly, savagely stabbing the ringer's calloused thumb – a callous developed from years of ringing, as a guitarist develops from years of playing chords.

The smallest birds are always the most anxious and therefore angriest, their place in the universe already so attenuated, so unlikely.

I AM AWARE: that hands appraise separately and exceptionally, that smothering them in latex would only compromise the fluidity of their thoughts.

MY HANDS ARE NOT as benignant as the other silent processes – left idle, they become pernicious. Left idle, they exact small harms upon other parts of my body, upon each other.

In the hours before noon, I sit at my desk dabbing at the dust-and-hair-and-crumb-littered keyboard of my laptop with hesitation, demonstrating a chronic under-use of the potential of my first phalange and mesophalange and metaphalange. Far more often than the tips of my fingers touch the keys, the nails of my fingers grope for abrasions – old spots, damaged cuticles, the ragged line joining hair to scalp.

In the hours before noon, I sit at my desk pecking at the weakest points of my body, whittling away tiny pieces of my fabric.

MY DAD RARELY WORE gloves or goggles, masks or ear muffs. He resorted to a hard hat only when he had to work outside in the rain. Countless years of recovering from the countless minor injuries inflicted by his daily hewing left him indifferent to the probability of some kind of major, accumulative harm that might, in the future, be impossible to recover from.

JOHN JAMES AUDUBON, the first man to record having successfully banded a wild bird, is better known as the intrepid explorer and master illustrator responsible for *Birds of America* – a book that depicts, each at the size of life and in extraordinary detail, 435 different avian species.

After celebrating the return of his eastern phoebes in their silver bracelets, Audubon steadily became engrossed by his passion for painting birds. Though he was, for a while, a proficient business owner, in 1819 he was declared bank-rupt and briefly jailed – misfortunes he later attributed to his all-consuming obsession with his hobby. From 1820 onwards Audubon devoted himself to the magnificent project of illustrating every feathered creature in North America, from the red-throated loon to the yellow-faced siskin, through the sooty tern, the tufted puffin, the gray catbird and the fork-tailed flycatcher. For the best part of the following twenty years, he roamed the natural habitats of his adopted continent with a portfolio and a gun.

His name is now inextricably linked to conservation in spite of the fact that, during the years he worked on his book, he shot dead tens of thousands of birds. Audubon didn't care about the autonomous life of each individual eagle or tern or coot or chickadee; he cared principally and obsessively about the accuracy and beauty of his depictions. He even invented a system of stands and wires and pulleys as a means to contort his freshly killed feathered creatures back into animated positions – flying, landing, perching, roosting, swooping.

Birds of America, first published in 1838, is today one of the most exquisite, and most valuable, books in the world.

AND YET IT'S ALSO an unfinished project, an *unfinishable* project – like every model railway, its whole elaborate and elaborately perfected miniature universe that can only ever represent a moment in time, a fixed point of history. '[M]odellers', Stephen Knott writes, 'often have a variety of different projects that are left half-finished or are completed at different speeds: it is not always a case of finishing one thing and going on to the next.'

IN THE CENTURIES SINCE the first publication of Audubon's masterpiece, approximately 558 new species have been identified and accepted by the American Birding Association, and six of his painted birds have become extinct: the Carolina parakeet, the Labrador duck, the Eskimo curlew, the great auk, the pinnated grouse and the passenger pigeon.

AUDUBON, LIKE MY DAD, lived out his adult life as unencumbered by the probability of future harm as he was by the ethics of shooting beautiful creatures. He died at sixty-five, having lost every one of his teeth due to the neglect they suffered throughout the decades he spent valiantly roving forests, mountains, meadows, bayous and swamps without a toothbrush.

MY DAD LIVED one year longer than Audubon.

He died of a cancer conjured from the fine traces of toxins that accumulated in his lungs over the course of decades; which emanated from his daily bashing, clanging, whirring and grinding, and hovered in the air of his sheds – the unwanted produce of his progress, ungraspable yet ubiquitous as the sky in a model railway.

AT THE WAKE, a colleague of my mother's – a man I barely knew – clutched my right hand with both of his, one pressed against my palm, the other strangling my wrist, and proclaimed that my public display of grief was insufficient:

It hasn't really hit you yet, he told me. It's going to really hit you later.

I HAVE A GENERAL INTEREST in the ages people die at, and how.

My granddad, my dad's dad, lived to be five years older than Audubon, and four years older than his son, dying of heart failure with all of his teeth and both lungs intact. He was a quiet, unfussy man and he had a quiet, unfussy death — a sudden death, and so he must surely have left behind unfinished projects.

MY GRANDDAD HAD a workshop in his attic.

I remember: the smell of pine and varnish, a saw bench in the middle of the room, wood dust glittering chimerically in a shaft of light. In his workshop, my granddad made wood-turned bowls and tiny boxes, but his principal projects were model horse-drawn carts, one of which is displayed on the top shelf of the dresser in my parents' house, extending across most of the full length of the fretwork and consisting of hundreds of individual parts: short strips of brass and thin cuts of wood and then the tens of tiny fittings that hold it together – rivets, pins, joints and chains.

The horse cart's wheels are tightly screwed onto its mahogany stand – it has been built scrupulously, in order that it might never enact the function it simulates. There is no miniature cart horse to harness it to, no harness, and nobody has taken it down from the dresser in several years.

THE ATTIC WORKSHOP was inside the roof of a small terraced house in Thirsk, a market town in North Yorkshire, the home of James Herriot. The small plot his small house sat upon was the only patch of land my granddad ever owned. His own dad had suffered a gas attack in the trenches of the First World War and, due to the long-term effects, died when he was only in his early forties. His widow felt she had no choice but to send her two sons away to work on the land, and so my granddad was a farm labourer from early on in life – he experienced firsthand the last era in which horse carts were in common use throughout the English countryside.

When war broke out again in 1939, he was eighteen. As a skilled agricultural worker, he was automatically exempt from conscription. In return for the misfortune of his boyhood, my granddad got a chance to survive the War, to marry, to father three sons, to move to town and hollow out a workshop in the attic of his house, and to furnish it gradually with the tools of his chosen craft – bench, lathe, saw, chisel, spindle, gouge.

I WAS SIX when my granddad died and I remember him only barely. It's bittersweet but fair to say that the horse cart on the dresser made a more lasting impression on my childhood than the man who had built it.

In my parents' house, there are a small number of objects whose hallowed value I have always been aware of: an antique music box, a llama-wool tapestry, the leather-bound uncut first edition of *The King of Elfland's Daughter* by Lord Dunsany. The horse cart is the only one that comes from my dad's side of the family and the only one made by an actual relative. As a child, I reserved a special kind of awe for this object; I thought of it as a sculpture – as a masterpiece – but later on, when I became an art student, I realised it wasn't the work of my granddad in the sense I'd always assumed; that he hadn't invented and designed it, but simply followed someone else's plan in a book of plans aimed at the market in amateur craft.

My granddad's horse carts – there are at least seven, as it turns out, scattered between relatives in England – are based on designs by a man called John Thompson, from a book called *Making Model Horse-Drawn Vehicles*, first published in 1976.

The horse cart was preordained by a stranger, I realised, and multiple other identical horse carts, assembled by strangers, exist simultaneously in the world beyond my mum's dresser.

As the illusion of the object's originality dissolved, so did my awe. As a cynical art student, I felt betrayed by my long-dead granddad, at first, and then I felt superior.

IN *THE CRAFTSMAN*, Sennett is a little grumpy about the prospect of confronting the question 'What is art?' Instead, he sets out his inquiry as: 'We are trying to figure out what autonomy means — autonomy as a drive from within that impels us to work in an expressive way, by ourselves.'

MY GRANDDAD'S HORSE CARTS were full of wistfulness – for lapsed traditions and lost countryside. The Dutch artist Willem van Genk, born a few years after my granddad, was also interested in vehicles and their mechanisms, but most of all he was obsessed by the complex transport networks of big cities – by aeroplanes, zeppelins, cars, trucks, buses and trains – and by the systems that support them, and the traffic they create.

When van Genk was a child, he showed a talent for art, and practically nothing else. His mother died when he was very young; his father used to beat him because he was terrible at schoolwork. When van Genk was in his teens, he was removed from his family and placed into an orphanage. But in 1958, his luck changed when he was accepted by the Royal Academy for Visual Arts in The Hague. The director recognised something unique in his artwork and his approach – something apart. While van Genk was allowed to attend classes at the Academy, the director insisted that he paint whatever he felt like; that he follow his own inner guide. His compositions were often divided into panels and each panel crammed with a smaller scene – as if in an attempt to contain all of the separate things going on in the crowded cities and in his crowded mind at once. Similar in format to comic strips, but vastly different in content and feeling, his paintings are intricate and discomposed, replete with awkwardness and distress.

While the other students in the Academy were obliged to follow directions and complete exams, van Genk was exempt from the formal protocols – instead, it was accepted that his work was exceptional in some abstruse sense, that he was a visionary.

Because van Genk was a difficult man, because his behaviour was often irksome and ugly, because he was diagnosed as schizophrenic, he is generally classified as an outsider artist. And yet, he read widely; he was interested in history and politics, and he travelled – to Moscow, Paris, Rome, Madrid, Copenhagen and Prague, many of the great cities of Europe.

AT SOME POINT in the 1980s, van Genk set to work on a series of model trolleybuses. He would begin by fashioning a skeleton, then he would build up the flesh of the tram with found materials – tin, card, plastic, foil, string, glue – and finally he would collage the outermost layer with advertisements snipped out of magazines – for Pepsi and McDonald's, Aquafresh and Chocolat Extra Fin.

Seventy trolleybuses survive. They are monstrous when compared to model trains – the length of a small dog, the wingspan of a carrion crow; he was able to cradle them in his lap as he worked. Van Genk used to refer to himself as the 'King of Stations' but for the latter decades of his life he remained nearly always stationed in the apartment he had inherited from his sister in The Hague, and by the time he was forcibly removed from it and institutionalised in 1998, the entire living room floor had been taken over by a sprawling model trolleybus station – unfinished, of course.

Unlike the process of painting, which van Genk found endlessly frustrating and disappointing, he enjoyed making his trolleybuses.

IT WASN'T UNTIL several years after I'd finished art college that I finally bought a copy of *Making Model Horse-Drawn Vehicles*. Though the manual provided detailed drawings and plans, I found that there had never been any parts or kits to accompany it – my granddad had had to source, cut, shape, place, affix and varnish every individual, finicky piece himself.

He had put in an awful lot of hours, I realised; he had paid attention and taken pains. But he had also clearly derived contentment – from the satisfaction of making well and from an object well made – and all of this experience – these feelings – had been nailed into the pine of his completed horse carts: tens of tiny brass fittings as well as the maker's bottomless patience, his particular skills, his style.

I remember: my granddad, in his workshop in the attic, the space he hollowed out for himself, surrounded by a nimbus of glittering dust.

'WE MUST BEGIN', William Morris said in his lecture 'Useful Work v. Useless Toil' to the Hampstead Liberal Club in 1884, 'to build up the ornamental part of life.'

IN THE YEARS SINCE my dad died, I have wondered why he didn't inherit his own dad's inclination for decoration.

My mum tells me that he owned a couple of books about wrought iron. In the shelves of the dresser beneath the horse cart I find *The Blacksmith's Craft: An Introduction to Smithing for Apprentices and Craftsmen* and *Decorative Ironwork* – both published in the UK by the Council for Small Industries in Rural Areas. If he had lived longer – if he had reached a state at which he lacked the stamina for power tools, for the cold of the shed in winter – would he have downsized his tools of metallurgy, I wonder now, cleared out the attic and become a hobbyist?

The word 'wrought' comes from the old English for 'work', the medieval past tense of its verb.

Or maybe it skipped a generation: the devotion to useless, beautiful objects, to the ornamental part of life – from my granddad directly down to me.

EVERY TIME I VISIT my parents' house, I go upstairs to my old bedroom. I meet again: the fimo elephant, the polystyrene robins, the knitted fish and all of their comrades. Everybody else also possesses these kinds of miniatures, I am presuming – that the world is stuffed with childhood compendiums in every conceivable and inconceivable permutation – and I am curious as to why everybody else doesn't continue to amass them, as I do.

I would like to know at what stage of life a person stops making small, painted objects, and how I managed to overshoot it.

THIS SUMMER, Mark and I make a renewed effort with the songbirds.

We realise the feeder should be closer to some shrubbery – that without the shelter of a network of slim, densely spaced branches within easy-retreating distance, the finches, tits and sparrows are understandably reluctant to expose themselves to passing hawks. The smallest of the songbirds, we realise, live with the nonstop fear of being ambushed. I buy a new feeder from the garden centre and Mark transforms an old timber pallet into a ladder and scales the rock slope behind the house. Atop the rock, along the perimeter of the cow field, fuchsia, gorse and blackberry brambles tangle together into a deranged kind of hedge. Mark singles out a fattish twig and fastens the feeder to it, as securely as possible.

It dangles within clear sight of the kitchen window, and so, every time we need to use the sink, we linger, we check the feeder.

RINSING PLATES, mugs, spoons, hands, wounds, we check the feeder.

Filling glasses, kettles, vases, pans, we check the feeder.

We check the feeder. We check the feeder. We check the feeder.

THE LEVEL OF THE SEED starts to drop, after a few days, though neither of us has witnessed any finches, sparrows or tits, and a channel opens up through the grass beneath the hedge – a tunnel the width of a plum – and after a few days more, we see the rat. He sits at the very edge clutching a sunflower seed between his front paws. He finishes the seed, discards the shell and reaches up to the lip of the feeder – unsnarling, elongating himself like an acrobat, almost falling.

The same rat, we assume, who ate a hole in the rubber foot of Mark's waders, who chewed away the foam handlebars of my mountain bike – always the same acrobat rat, even though, of course, there must be hundreds.

THIS SUMMER, on a fine day close to its end, I find a row of picnic benches along a harbour front, each painted the shade of a nursery wall – pale purple, pastel green, balmy yellow, subdued blue – and bolted into the granite. A woman sits in the unlikely sun, alone on her bench, alone on the whole row of benches, facing out to sea but with some papers opened beside her, some kind of a drawing or plan.

House sparrows hop on the slabs, patrolling for crumbs.

The woman is knitting – a wide, bobbled garment, watermelon pink; her long needles ticking, glinting.

I APPROACH THE KNITTER, smile and say it's nice to see someone knitting, that this is something I never seem to see anymore. She flicks out the tail of her garment and explains it's a baby blanket that will be a gift for her not-yet-born niece, that she's following a pattern from the papers beside her. Then she takes out her phone and opens up photographs of the other things she has made, other garments, other gifts – a set of 'sweetie' jars with frilly lids; a cross-stitch birthday card; a pair of fairy wings hemmed with pinprick lights; a chocolate bonsai tree; a long, silk, teal dress. Every Christmas, the knitter says, she makes the same gift for her daughter – an embroidered stocking. And it takes so long to finish, she says, that she must begin embroidering in the summer; she must commit half of every year to the preparation of a single present – and though it will always take the form of a stocking, each year she slightly alters the design – in this way, making it more interesting for herself, she says – staving off the gnaw of boredom.

She makes the things she makes in the evenings, in front of the television.

AND EVERYONE at the party, the knitter says, complimented my dress, asking where I had bought it — as if the teal silk which she had sewn herself, which she had fingered all over — had an ambiguous radiance that the shop-bought dresses lacked.

WILLIAM MORRIS — artist, designer, writer, activist, socialist — agreed that hands know what they must do without instruction, that the objects shaped by their ancestor's phalanxes and phalanges and metacarpals for thousands of years remain in the memory compartment of their tiny brains, in the same way as birds know which way to fly without being guided or following a plotted course, without a book that provides detailed drawings and plans with parts and kits to accompany it.

'[N]o man, however original he may be', Morris writes in *The Lesser Arts*, 'can sit down day-to-day and draw the ornament of a cloth, or the form of an ordinary vessel or a piece of furniture, that will be other than a development or a degradation of forms used hundreds of years ago; and these, too, very often, forms that once had a serious meaning, though they are now become little more than a habit of the hand; forms that were once perhaps the mysterious symbols of worships and beliefs now little remembered or wholly forgotten.'

He was a wealthy man, an intellectual, and yet Morris chose his workshop over and above his desk; he was more likely to be found wearing a dye-stained smock than the velveteen smoking jacket of a Victorian gentleman. In

The Arts and Crafts Movement in Britain, Mary Greensted described him as short, stocky and extravagantly bearded, in a bright blue fisherman's shirt and a soft, battered hat.

I consider myself a disciple of Morris – for his doctrine of truth to nature and to materials, and to people. Art must arise from daily life, he believed, and the person who labours must be inseparable from the product of their labour – it must synchronously be a product of their will, their pains, their talents, their tenderness.

HIS DESIGNS — for textiles, wallpaper, books and glass — are dense in detail yet deceptively simple. There are often small birds, though it may take a moment for the eye to single them out amid his luscious flowers and intertwined tendrils.

Inside Morris's arabesques, whimsical new species have found sanctuary.

MORRIS WAS INFLUENCED by traditional Islamic art, partly for the reason that craftwork like pottery, carpet-weaving, calligraphy and embroidery are conferred an equal status to painting and sculpture, and partly because in the Islamic tradition it is considered less important to replicate the details of nature than it is to convey their essence.

In the Islamic tradition, every pattern is sourced in the sacred, and every person in the workshop is trained with equal emphasis placed upon becoming a skilled artisan and becoming a decent, whole person – disciplined, humane, spiritual.

MY GRANDDAD MIGHT have been a disciple too – had I been old enough to understand Morris and his influences and to mention it during his lifetime; my dad too – if he'd been the kind of dad I'd had bookish, pedantic conversations with.

What did we talk about, my dad and I?

The different kinds of plyboard and woodworking joints, the correct way to change the bit of a drill and to hold and level and aim the gun of the welder, how to tell when a tyre has gone bald – and then he would always want to know whether or not I was doing okay for money.

WHAT WE ALL SHARED — me, my dad, his dad — was a suspicion of modern life, a loathing of fashion, a disappointment with the new technologies and a preference for the ad hoc contraptions of the past — anything that can be disassembled and reassembled with hands and tools, based upon the principles of common sense.

Each in our own time, we lived and live in consonance with nostalgia for a former one.

IF MY GRANDDAD WAS wood and my dad was iron, then what am I?

Though I share their affection for elemental materials, I get waylaid in the Art & Hobby shop, returning home with sacks of air-drying clay and modelling plaster, with bumper-packs of lollipop sticks, felt and cork and balsa. As a promising experiment becomes an object, as the object is multiplied, as the multiplicity of objects becomes a project, I graduate to the DIY store, for dowels and plyboard and sandpaper, for tubes of wood-glue and rolls of No-More-Nails tape and great tubs of emulsion paint: matt, flat-matt, satin, silk, soft-sheen, eggshell, gloss, high gloss – buff-breasted, bearded, crested, capped.

THIS HOUSE OF INDUSTRY is also a house of storage.

CONSTANTLY SUSCEPTIBLE to the possibility of future projects, I stockpile remnants on a weekly if not daily basis – the ambiguously interesting by-products of ordinary life dispatched by the ordinary universe and placed in my path like gentle prompts. The guest bedroom is the natural depository for these items of as-yet-unresolved fate, for this collection of possibilities. Here are the juveniles who won't survive their first migration in spite of the extensive efforts made on behalf of their new life, in spite of the great expectations.

MARK EXERCISES SUPERIOR self-control when confronted with the universe's unremitting dispatches — he is responsible for a far smaller measure of the collection.

If put to the test, any reasonable house guest would struggle to guess which items originated with whom, but between us there is never any confusion.

We each have our own vocabulary of materials. He is papers, shards of coloured plastic, bottletops, feathers, beads. I am tin-cans, sticks, timber offcuts, quick-drying cement, yoghurt pots. We overlap in the case of textiles, but where he is thread and ribbons and strings, I am samplers, rags and swatches.

He is fish, and I am birds.

IN THE LATEST STAGE of the evening, in the aftermath of the dusk walk and the preamble to dinner, we sit at opposite ends of the living-room table, facing each other but with eyes cast down, and talking in bursts, me always a little bit more than him, in the same way I own a little bit more stuff, in the same way I take up a little bit more space.

MARK MAKES DRAWINGS, but never in the living room, only ever alone and out of sight. In the latest stage of the evening, at his living-room-table station, he prepares fishing gear. The materials he uses could easily be mistaken for the materials of burgeoning art: dyed feathers, sequins, cat-gut, the empty cartridges of party-poppers, teardrops of lead, segments of light wood, fluorescent paint. They are becoming traces, rigs, lures and floats, and though he could easily buy them off the shelf from a tackle shop, he always chooses to make them himself from scratch, partly to save money, partly as a means of compensating for the shortfalls of the readymade market, and partly because he enjoys the challenge of adapting and customising: the contentment of making, the gratification of a trace or rig or lure or float well made.

Mark measures monofilament against his own arm span – rising suddenly from his station and holding them open, tugging the translucent line taut between each hand. This is how he can be sure he has a length of six feet.

HE STRINGS A LINE of strong twine between the roof of the garden shed and the fattish branch of the hedge above the rock bank along the hem of the field – and I slide the feeder away from the rat's tunnel, toward the shed but still as much as possible in the lee of the fuchsia and gorse and blackberry brambles – the sheltering shrubbery – out of the wind, at once both relatively prominent and relatively safe.

I HAVE BEEN mostly plaster, this year.

At the eastern end of the living-room table, I have sat for hours passing hard, white lumps between my hands.

And sometimes it seems as if I might have begun by plunging my fists into the walls that enclose me – as if the plaster I carve had been pulled straight from the fabric of this house.

THIS HOUSE OF STORAGE also stores objects and devices invented and assembled but ultimately discarded – condemned to prowl the shadowy nooks, the cracks in between shelved books, the crooks of the windowsills, the precipices of the mantelpieces. Dust-encrusted, rusted, warped, faded – these are the embodiment of failed visions, the ghosts of unrealised art, the products of experiments unpromising.

If each small object were a migrant bird and their congregation an installation, then these would be my vagrants – sundered from their fellow species, or more likely, lone members of uncompleted flocks.

THE KNITTER ALWAYS MAKES mistakes, she had told me on the sea front, in the earliest lines of a new knitted garment – and sometimes she pushes on, covering a substantial quantity of ground before noticing. No one else would even realise, she explained, but as soon as I see the mistake – as soon as I know that it's there – I must go back and fix it. I must unpick the whole lot; I must start over again.

The knitter has now accepted, she had said, that every new thing will begin with at least one false start.

THE MIGRATING BIRDS who come together into flocks in advance of departure will sometimes line up, assuming a soldier-like formation, and so there has to be one who rises first – who causes all of the others to follow – but even the experts are unclear on the precise status of the starting bird. It may be an elder, they say, but it's as likely to be a skittish, impatient juvenile who makes a false start, and spooks all of the others into following suit.

THERE ARE ALWAYS test-pieces – only one or two if I'm lucky, but a dozen is more usual.

Last spring, after I had carved 100 plaster objects, a single day devoted to each one, I started to carve them in a slightly different style – a slightly sharper, odder style – and after a while it became clear that the first hundred were inadequate; that the price of getting a single object right was 100 discarded objects and 100 days, an entire winter.

I TRIED TO REASON that I was wrong. I scrabbled for solutions, but once an object is contaminated, there is no means, no hope, of repair.

IN DISGUST, I sat on the floor and separated the tainted objects from those as-yet-untainted. I packed all of the hand-carved, palm-sized rejects into cardboard boxes collected from the stack behind the supermarket checkouts – boxes that had been designed specifically, so the information stickers read, for the transportation of plastic punnets of cherry tomatoes from Saudi Arabia to Skibbereen. In place of a lid, I shielded them in sheets of dismembered newspaper and slid them under the bed in the guest room and didn't even tell Mark what I had done.

I clipped their wings, placed them out of sight, and started over again.

TWITCHERS TRAVEL the world just to sight new species.

To the water-logged pastures of Cambodia for a gigantic ibis; to the clammy rainforests of southern Sumatra for a cuckoo who lives on the ground; to the islands of the Philippines for a monkey-eating eagle, and to the archipelago of New Caledonia for a bird that is not quite an owlet and not quite a nightjar, and that hasn't been spotted alive for two decades.

But I am less concerned by the birds of foreign grounds and trees and skies, of elsewhere. The birds I want to see, the birds I want to learn to recognise, are the ones that live – or visit, or get lost – in the places where I live –

my grounds, my trees, my skies.

I am concerned, fundamentally, with my daily birds.

WHEN I START PREPARING a new object, it's with a picture in my mind.

Though I am also guided by reading and research, by thinking and reasoning – primarily I am guided by the picture.

The picture is my destination, and everything else is an interesting peregrination, and every object successfully completed is a reunion – with the picture in my mind when I began. If I don't experience this sense of reunion on completion of a test-piece, it is instantly discarded. But then there are the times at which I am not so certain; the times at which it takes 100 tests and several wasted weeks before it dawns on me that I am going backwards.

THE BIRDS WHO CROSS great oceans have no gauge for measuring distance travelled; they can only determine where they are based on the amount of time that has passed. Some of them, the birders say, are able to read the surface of the sea as if it were a map.

A map of no obvious contours or symbols.

A massive, restless, churning map – its marks heavily congested, hieroglyphic.

I ASK MARK if fish read the bed of the sea, like birds read its surface, but he doesn't know, and doesn't bother to make something up – drawing from a loosely related fact, stretching it out with right-sounding ideas, elaborating and embellishing – as I would.

THE AGONY OF THE discarded objects comes not from the waste of matter but the monstrous loss of time – time that had been meticulously embodied only to vanish at the instant an object is rejected. What it means is that my efforts will not be wholly reflected by my output, and this gives way to the most profound of my concerns – that it will not show through, in the finished artwork, how much and how acutely I care.

I CARE, ACUTELY.

In the sculpture department of the art college where I studied, the works I finished were self-conscious, ironic, novel, but the tutors were sympathetic. They saw how much time I spent there; they saw the proof of my efforts on the pages of my notebooks and the narrow expanses of wall that surrounded my studio desk. They rewarded my conviction with the good grades my finished pieces were never worthy of.

I CARE, ACUTELY.

When a bit breaks off, as bits often do, I hear myself cry
out, as involuntarily as if it was a part of my body that had
snapped, not a nub of plaster, a dropped stitch, but a slip
of skin shucked from a knuckle, a nick of cartilage, a chip
of bone.

IF WHAT DISTURBS ME about the discarded objects is the loss of time they represent, then what concerns me, in the execution of objects, is how I can show, in material form, all the immaterial hours that have passed into each – the parade of ideas, the *ad infinitum* intentions – 'the thousand little everyday moves', Richard Sennett writes, 'that add up in sum to a practice'.

THE BIRD WHO MAKES the longest journey of migration is the Arctic tern. A study from 2015–16 found that the birds who breed on the Farne Islands off the coast of Northumberland fly up to 96,000 kilometres down the west coast of Africa, and over the Southern Ocean to Antarctica, and then back again – across cliffs and islands, blue whales and leopard seals, great garbage patches and billions of tonnes of krill – re-fashioning their route constantly, re-setting their compass in accordance with the changing winds – and yet still it is impossible to say whether the Arctic tern's year is ultimately made easier by going the indirect way, or more difficult.

She is the creature who experiences the most daylight – zig-zagging away her short life in a world of perpetual summer.

BY AUTUMN, I have sighted, in the garden: a pied wagtail skirting the base of the wall, a blackbird gouging a crack in the path, a pair of choughs – one on each gate post – several herring gulls and several more hooded crows. I pick, out of the overgrown lawn: a grey feather, a black feather, a white feather, and place them in a vase – a monochrome bouquet, ironed flat. Only the robin brings some colour, the same robin at every different stage of light.

The seed rattling in the feeder, swaying on the line beyond the kitchen window, bloats up with rain and starts to rot.

The yellowish, greenish, blueish, pinkish, purpleish birds – elsewhere entrenched in their routines – refuse to be tempted.

WE DRIVE A METAL POLE deep into the wild rose bush in the sod of the centre of the lawn, and wrench the feeder from its line, and attach it to the pole, with nails and twine, old hair bobbles, even cable-ties – the kind of fasteners that the wind would need fingernails to undo.

IN THE LATTER STAGES of the nineteenth century, the members of the Arts and Crafts Movement took care to leave the signature of the maker's hand behind on each individual piece. 'Constructional details', Mary Greensted writes, 'such as through tenons and dovetails were exposed in woodworking, while hand-raised silverwork was left with the marks of the hammer.'

The surface of each piece of furniture, jewellery, cutlery and ware was a map – of marks heavily congested, hiero-glyphic.

John Paul Cooper, an architect and craftsman in jewellery and metalwork was, according to Greensted, driven 'by the idea that inanimate objects had an inner spirit which could be brought to life by the artist'.

NARROW BLADES CUT scant scrapes, nipped brushes sketch slim strokes, fine needles pull tight stitches – numberless gentle marks accumulate into a whole, small object; many small, whole objects of numberless gentle marks come together into a significant installation, like the legion of small flaps that add up in sum to a magnificent journey – this is the model by which I work.

KEEPING CLOSE but casually ignoring the tools of measurement – ruler, tape, level, compass, scales – I appraise and estimate by eye and by hand –

I chip, I scratch, I dab, I pat, I prick; touching every part of every object at every stage in every state; favouring a quality of mark that denotes uncertainty and anxiety as opposed to confidence and serenity; favouring a human scale, a humane scale, a physically-possible-alone-scale. 'Men were not meant', Ruskin writes, 'to work with the accuracy of tools', and so each installation must stop at the size that can be achieved by a single human being working alone – no higher than I can reach, no faster than I can fly.

Touch by touch by touch, hesitation by hesitation by hesitation, because *this* and *this* and *this* is how acutely I care.

AS MUCH AS I LOVE materiality, I hate materialism.

And try, at every opportunity, to avoid buying plastic articles mass-produced for the overstuffed planet. Instead, I haunt the charity shops and car boot sales and flea markets – because I want to believe that each thing I own has at least one story older and other than the one I will give it. Amongst my belongings: a sloppy oil painting of a bouquet of white carnations signed *Caroline, March 7th, 1997*, a buttercup-yellow jumper with a label sewn into the collar which spells out the name: *DARYL JACKSON*.

A couple of flannel sheets – bobbled.

Several novelty mugs – chipped.

The semaphore signal from a model railway – its miniature metal arm fractured.

I AM AWARE OF – I am sensitive to – the means by which my daily handiwork breaches this principle.

And so I search for ways to exonerate the items I make afresh and the waste created along the byways of their making – the shavings of carved plaster and the dust of sanded wood, the paint that crusts on my palette, the sheets and sheets of soiled kitchen roll, the blobs and blobs of dried super glue, the jars and jars of cloudy water.

I search for a new principle by which to justify my daily waste.

IF ALL OF THESE MATERIALS already exist, perhaps it can be that I am liberating and transforming them from a collection of banal scattered matter into art. Because objects have a stringent class system – governed by the quality of their story, and by how much care has gone in to their making, and by how much they are cared for as a belonging.

'THE GENUINENESS of a thing', Walter Benjamin writes in *The Work of Art in the Age of Mechanical Reproduction*, 'is the quintessence of everything about it since its creation that can be handed down from its material duration to the historical witness that it bears.' He describes the 'aura' of a historical object as 'a unique manifestation of a remoteness, however close it may be', and Celeste Olalquiaga in *The Artificial Kingdom: A Treasury of the Kitsch Experience* describes it as 'a metaphysical halo that surrounds certain experiences and things, giving them an invisible glow'.

THE BUTTERCUP-YELLOW JUMPER, balled up at the bottom of the laundry basket – food-spattered, sweat-scented – and the dust-misted carnations of the charity shop painting, its scuffed frame; Daryl and Caroline for a moment in time, almost imperceptibly, glow – and my mum's photo frame of my dad's inconspicuous creations, and the vagrant artworks lurking in nooks and cracks and crooks, sills and precipices – and every silent flap – all in their silent radiance.

I FLAIL FOR SMALL absolutions, but I am Audubon — caring chiefly and obsessively not about nature but the accuracy and beauty of its depiction – not the living world, but its lifeless replication.

Inch by inch, I am making a lifeless replication of the world I know – this is the model by which I work.

MY DAILY HANDIWORK takes its toll on the house as it does my body, as it does the planet – the ubiquitous dust and displaced particles, the splashes and stab marks, the spotted prints of white paint passed from my fingers and palms to the black plastic of the electric kettle, to the drinking glasses, the mugs, the tap, the handle of the oven door, the stove door, the fridge door. The stamp of old squeezes, my daily clasping – they appear so subtly and so gradually I don't even notice.

THERE ARE TOKEN GESTURES I make to protect the house, as there are to protect my organs, as there are to protect the planet.

There are strokes of wiping, strokes of brushing, strokes of sweeping; a special cloth for the surface of the mixing station, a different special cloth for soaking the water out of soiled bristles. There is the scraping of plaster scum off each used blade with a blade unused, unscummed, and a broom to reach beneath the eastern end of the living room table, across the hearth rug to the skirting board, back and forth across the worn linoleum, back and forth.

There are flourishes of rinsing; every practice always ends in a rinsing.

THERE IS A MODEL TRAIN circling a diorama in a glass case in a train station in a small city somewhere in western Germany – through the balsa and fibreglass and latex landscape, around and around its single track – circling, chuffing, chiming.

EVERY MORNING, I place everything out in preparation for the day. Every night, I tidy up, and place everything away in preparation for the next day.

I put things out, I tidy up, I put things away.

I prepare, I prepare, I prepare.

SOMETIMES, I LOOK BACK and wonder how much of the time I think I spend making – how much of the time I claim to spend making – is actually devoted to the organisation and reorganisation of necessary elements.

Sometimes, I look back and wonder why there seems to be so little, so crushingly little, and I struggle to fully believe – to fully accept – that just *this*, *this* and *this* is where the countless hours went – the countless gestures and strokes and flourishes, the countless thoughts and decisions and preparations.

I BELIEVE it does not matter at all; I believe it is all that matters.

AND YET, THERE MUST always come, at some stage, the finishing point with its pure joy, for though flow is transiently sublime, this is the true sublime – finishing.

'ORIGINALITY IS A MARKER OF TIME,' Richard Sennett writes, 'it denotes the *sudden* appearance of something where before there was nothing, and because something suddenly comes into existence, it arouses in us emotions of wonder and awe.'

THE WONDER AND AWE, the catharsis and reassurance – the guilty bliss – of a fresh small object placed into the world; some entirely unique, inimitable thing that didn't exist just a couple of hours ago, and which I have brought into existence myself – alone and utterly. A trail of progress I can see; I can feel; I can place; I can move around in a shaft of light; I can hold aloft to the damaged planet. What the day before yesterday was water and dust was yesterday a mould and today is an art object – this is my daily magic.

SOLID OBJECTS and the solidification of time they represent effect a more solid kind of joy, whereas my writing is so eagerly wounded, so easily destroyed. One coffee cup spilled across the keyboard of my laptop, and hundreds of thousands of assiduously aligned words are instantly lost, whereas it would take some physical effort to reckon away the box-room of art, some tools of demolition.

And even then it would still, in some sense, in its fragments, be there. A collection of elements, a mess of rubble, which bear the mark of my physical efforts and blind faith.

AND AFTER the finishing point, what then?

THEN I SWITCH the lights on in the morning, un-ball my socks, brush my teeth, lift mugs and bowls and plates out of cupboards and drawers and off hooks, chop and fry and toss vegetables, send emails, wash my hands, put mugs and bowls and plates back into cupboards and drawers and onto hooks and reply to emails. Then I ball my socks up again at night.

I switch off the lights.

'ALL THE WHILE nature will go on', William Morris writes, 'with her eternal recurrence of lovely changes – spring, summer, autumn and winter; sunshine, rain, and snow; storm and fair weather; dawn, noon, and sunset; day and night.'

TOGETHER WITH MARK, I gather every small, hand-formed, hand-painted object into a flock; we measure and weigh and calculate; we secure a ring around every bony ankle.

WE GO TO THE BARGAIN SHOP and buy twelve rolls of quilted toilet paper and eleven long, deep boxes of rigid plastic.

We go to the supermarket, to the spot behind the checkouts, and we take every box from the stack. They are corrugated card, sepia brown – strong enough to support separated-out apples and lettuces, cartons of mushrooms and packets of herbs, bundled leeks and beets and chard – from Kenya and Columbia, Ghana and Guatemala, Israel, Egypt, Zambia.

We go to the newsagents and ask for old newspapers; we go to the electrical shop and ask for old polystyrene; we go to the fine art framers and ask for old bubblewrap.

We go to the shoe shop in pursuit of a lighter kind of box with a readymade lid.

We make a final trip back down the main street to the place where the van is parked, each with a tower of shoeboxes balanced between the tips of our fingers and the tips of our chins.

BACK AGAIN IN THE HOUSE, we designate new stations. The kitchen worktop, the living room floor and out into the hallway. Mark is slicing the heavy card with a Stanley blade and a steel ruler, constructing a system of compartments inside the plastic boxes – a bed of polystyrene, a grid of narrow rooms with slotting walls. I am folding and stapling bubblewrap envelopes – one for every small painted object, of which there are hundreds. I am lining the narrow rooms with scrumpled newspaper and crushed toilet-roll; I am swaddling, padding, nestling, tucking.

A tarnished kind of snow starts to collect – brittle brown ribbons, the dust of sundered paper fibres, the white flakes of shaved polystyrene.

AND WHEN IT RUNS OUT — all of the packing materials we gathered — we resort to the shelves of the hot-press, for the bath-mats and fleecy dog blankets with their patterns of zig-zags and cartoon paw prints. We press them down into the boxes, prod them around the unbuffered edges of the wrapped plates — softly, softly — even though, at this stage, we are both so sick and tired of being careful.

FINALLY, I MAKE LABELS — in black felt-tip, with a phone number, a destination; with the appropriate orientation; with an indication of whether each box is HEAVY or LIGHT.

I sellotape them to every side.

I AM TOUCHED – by the time Mark devotes to this, my task; by the several days he allows to be lost to his own work. I am touched – by the frustration he suffers on my behalf.

He does it partly out of love, or so I imagine, and partly out of obligation, but mostly out of his own deep-rooted solicitude. Mark is chronically incapable of executing an important task crudely or inadequately and then continuing blithely on with the ordinary days, undaunted by the memory of a past shortcoming.

He would be the one to lie awake at night – envisioning the rectangle of cardboard that didn't quite fit, the sheet of tissue paper insufficiently scrunched.

The main source of his frustration: that he must handle my task in ways he never would his own work, for himself. He doesn't feel good, for example, about the final number of boxes.

I would never normally do things in elevens, he says.

I EXPECT TO BE RELIEVED, once it is all boxed; instead I am outstandingly lonely – for the out-of-sight objects themselves, but more specifically, more severely – for the bump-bump-bump and the scrape-scrape-scrape and the dab-dab-dab; for the preparations.

I must restrain myself from peeling the plastic lids back off their plastic coffins; I must persuade myself to resist removing every last small, hand-formed, hand-painted object from its custom-designed compartment – untucking, unnestling, unpadding, unswaddling – to touch them again, to touch them up again.

And up, and up, and up.

I EXPECTED TO BE RELIEVED, once it was all made.

This flock that I began after my dad died.

This making of the flock, which had for two years been fending off the awareness of his daily absence.

Instead I am outstandingly lonely.

WHAT DID WE even used to say to each other? I still have no idea about plyboard and joints and drill bits; I can't weld and my tyres are bald.

And I don't understand about money — where it comes from, how far it might go.

AN ISLAND ONE MILE WIDE and three miles long and eight miles from the mainland, the most southern point of Ireland, autumn.

A desperately unsmooth island, with too few mature trees and level surfaces; an island with a grotto, a lighthouse, a graveyard, a library-in-a-portacabin, a single shop-come-pub that keeps an entirely capricious schedule of opening hours – an island that decides when and what you eat and drink, or if you eat and drink at all.

Because they have refused to come to me, I have decided I must chase them.

FOR THE BIRDS, autumn is a season of serious activity.

As soon as the montbretia pitches out of the ditches and the ash leaves wrinkle and the wasp-eaten apples smash wetly against the slackening grass – so the migrant birds start to seek each other out again, to pick teams – the adults who know the way, the juveniles, many of whom will not survive their inaugural trip – getting caught up in storms or poisoned by agricultural pesticides; flying too fast and hard into buildings too tall, or the outstretched arms of pylons, the windscreens of planes, the propellers of wind turbines; running out of food, running out of energy, running out of habitats they once relied upon – pit stops once sustaining, now bulldozed, built-over, barren.

The starter birds – their chances of ultimately arriving only about as good and likely as those of all the starter artists.

AND THEN THERE ARE the resident birds who happened to fall in with a migrant flock of the same species over the course of the hazy, propitious summer – they will leave with their migratory comrades even though they are not supposed to, in an act of optimism, or perhaps confusion.

And lastly, there are the birds for whom this tiny island represents neither source nor destination but a layover along the route of a longer passage, a pearl in the necklace of a protracted flyway. Blackcaps, turtle doves, firecrests, whimbrels, ruffs – the passage migrants are impervious to the grotto, the lighthouse, the graveyard, the library-in-a-portacabin, the shop-come-pub. They stop for the insects that hatched in summer, for the weed that blooms in the emerald lake, for the smashed apples and the berries of cultivated cotoneaster, for the creatures that dwell in the festering seaweed above the shifting lines of the tide.

For the birds, autumn is a month of serious activity.

AND YOU WILL KNOW them by their colour and size and shape – the birders say – by the type of environment in which you find them and the rough time of year it is, by their song – but most of all, you will know them by their *jizz* – a style of flight, of hop, of perch; the way they hold their mortal parts and move; the way their small heads and limbs and wings interact with one another; with the world around them; with the ungraspable sky.

THERE IS A SMALL SONGBIRD, the northern wheatear. She weighs about as much as a small songbird – a pinch more than a robin and a few pinches less than a thrush – even though commentators always insist on making analogies with light objects one might more typically have cause to balance on the palm of a hand – a packet of crisps, a glass of water, a ball of wool, a fountain pen – or with the cost of an envelope that could be posted for the price of two standard stamps, or with the hypothetical weight of a human soul.

SHE TOPPLES OUT of the ditch in front of me — even though I am not searching for birds; I am not searching for poetic coincidences.

I have not brought my binoculars.

SHE TOPPLES OUT of the ditch in front of me — as I follow a narrow road, jogging, up a steep hill on the mile-wide island in the early morning, in the autumn. She hops up again and finds a perch in the brambles, twists her neck around and regards me, weighs me up with her black dot eyes — holding herself unnervingly still and for so long that I am the one who turns away.

From the pictures I have studied; from the distinctive 'T' of black fanning the tip of her white tail feathers, I am able to identify this bird as a northern wheatear, and when I describe the incident, later on in the day, to the warden at the bird observatory, he tells me it was probably a juvenile who arrived in the night from Greenland; that most likely I was the first human she had ever seen, and I find this both obvious and strangely surprising — that a bird might be as curious to look at me as I am to look at birds.

THERE IS A STORY from bird-lore about a skipper who believed he had hauled up from the stormy Atlantic in his fishing nets a flock of hibernating swallows. Clinging to the mesh with their tightly contracted toes and claws, their ink-blue wings seamlessly encasing every other distinguishing feature – head, neck and nape, bill, breast and belly – had hardened into teardrop-shaped, lightly striated shells.

They were each too small to be birds, but in the sky there are never enough objects together at once to produce a clear perception of scale; there is only the sense of pervading advance, pervading recession.

There are only the approaches.

AND SO TO A MAN in a trawler on the surface of the sea, a bird in the sky might be the size of a bird, or the size of a dog, or the size of a mussel shell.

ACCORDING TO BIRD-LORE, it's lucky to have swallows nesting on a property – and on my dad's property, a nook created by the intersection of his shed and the old greenhouse has, for thirty-four years, provided a sheltered space for storing the rubbish bins, the ash bucket, a big box of glass destined for the bottle-bank, and the nest of a European barn swallow – a half-hemisphere of caked mud, straw and sticks, the coarse hair of cows and the moulted down of hens.

According to bird-lore, my dad should have been a lucky man, but this was not how he felt at the very end of his life.

At the very end of his life, my dad concentrated his hands on fixing and arranging and rearranging; on making every necessary practical preparation for the handover of his material universe – his unlovely oeuvre of machinery, furniture, gates, paths and customised polytunnels – and as he worked he concentrated his mind on visions of how it would grow old – how it would rust and peel and break; how the weathered parts would come apart, and he would not be there to repair them.

At the very end of his life, my dad was visited by the 558 birds that Audubon missed, and every model railway uncompleted, and all the walnut, maple, cherry, elm, hickory and ash his own dad never turned, and the ironwork he would never hammer, roll, weld, pierce, twist – the heaps of blackened, puddled scrap that he would never re-handle into something ornamental, something beautiful.

ACCORDING TO BIRD-LORE, he should have been a lucky man, but luck follows no particular order. It has a starting point and a finishing point and it fluctuates. There are tailwinds of luck and headwinds of luck and cross-winds of luck – and the barn swallows who chose, year after year, to nest in the sheltered space created by the nook of his sheds may have spared my dad some greater kind of trauma – the slow loss of his mind, of his loved ones, the sixth mass extinction – his death may itself have been the luck they brought.

HE DIED IN THE EVENING, in early summer, when evening was just beginning to come late, and as he died I was restless, keen for the fuss to be ended so that I could be elsewhere; so that I could get on with my work.

I stepped outside, and sat on the bench he had built, in the yard between the shed and the studio he had built, beside the flowerbeds he had built, and a swallow swooped low across the yard, looped and left again, but seconds later, returned – swooped again, looped again, called.

AND IT SEEMED TO ME, then, both obvious and strangely surprising – how my world appears to order itself around these poetic coincidences, whether I search for them or not; how a planet so overstuffed and complicated can so keenly configure itself in response to my flights of thought, my flock of connections.

'TAKEN ALL TOGETHER', Jonathan Franzen writes in his essay 'The Radical Otherness of Birds', 'the flight paths of birds bind the planet together like 100bn filaments, tree to tree and continent to continent.'

'There was never a time when the world seemed large to them.'

I ALSO SPOT, on the mile-wide island in autumn: a fluffy pink starling, a songbird even lighter than a wren with a bright streak of yellow across its scalp, and a black seabird the size of a song thrush with ungainly webbed feet it uses to paddle on the surface of the water. They are the kinds of birds a child might invent; a child might make out of fimo, cardboard, polystyrene, tinfoil, wool – that would later turn out to be real.

They were my daily birds all along.

AT THE VERY END OF LIFE, what did my dad remember? No rose-coloured starlings, no goldcrests, no storm petrels, or so I imagine. No significant moments of transcendence, no significant moments of torment – no significant moments – only the things he did over, and over.

The glorious, crushing, ridiculous repetition of life.

WHEN THE EXHIBITION is ended —

I will go, alone, and take it down again.

I WILL DISMANTLE the installations, break each back into their many parts, wrap the parts and re-nestle them into their padded compartments. I will match small painted objects to envelopes, to boxes, to slots. I will re-pad, re-press and re-prod the bathmats and dog blankets, re-secure the lids of the rigid plastic boxes, all eleven, and affix new labels — the address of a destination in the opposite direction, of our house, this house.

And it will all go back the way it came, bearing a few specks of damage, the cost of its display, the autograph of its passage.

It will be winter then.

A HOUSE WHERE this dead twig might be for the fire, and this dead twig might be for whittling and sanding smooth, coating with metallic paint, collaging with paper leaves and planting into the summer green mat of a silver birch forest.

A HOUSE SYMPATHETIC to my preoccupations and repetitions and observances; a house whose walls and floors and furniture diligently, doggedly, interminably order themselves around my daily practices –

My daily handiwork.

A NOTE ON THE IMAGES

Each of the fourteen images included in this book depict a single model bird from a series that I started to build in the spring of 2019 and photographed in the autumn. They represent, in order of appearance: a northern wheatear, a pigeon, a sparrowhawk, a willow warbler, an albatross, an eastern phoebe, a swallow, a hooded crow, a chaffinch, an Arctic tern, a chough, a pied wagtail, a blackcap and an American redstart. Each is made from plaster that has been carved, painted and mounted onto a length of timber dowel, and studded with a pair of glass beads.

BIBLIOGRAPHY

Amateur Craft: History and Theory by Stephen Knott, Bloomsbury, 2015

The Craftsman by Richard Sennett, Penguin, 2009

On Longing: Narratives of the Miniature, the Gigantic, the Souvenir, the Collection by Susan Stewart, Duke University Press, 1993

Adhocism: The Case for Improvisation by Charles Jencks and Nathan Silver, expanded and updated edition, The MIT Press, 2013

Living on the Wind: Across the Hemisphere with Migratory Birds by Scott Weidensaul, North Point Press, 1999

The Cave by José Saramago, translated by Margaret Jull Costa, Vintage, 2003

Useful Work versus Useless Toil by William Morris, Penguin, 2008

The Arts and Crafts Movement in Britain by Mary Greensted, Shire Publications, 2010

The Work of Art in the Age of Mechanical Reproduction by Walter Benjamin, translated by J.A. Underwood, Penguin, 2008

The Artificial Kingdom: A Treasury of the Kitsch Experience by Celeste Olalquiaga, Bloomsbury, 1999

I have also included a quote from an essay by Jonathan Franzen entitled 'The Radical Otherness of Birds', which was published in *The Guardian*, 23 March 2018.

ACKNOWLEDGEMENTS

This little book was written incrementally over the course of 2018. It came about partly as a response to the process of building three sculptural installations that were exhibited together in a solo show in the Morley Gallery in central London in the autumn of that year. My thanks to Morley College and Culture Ireland for making the show possible, and to Simrath Panaser, the curator who initially invited me to exhibit. The books and essays she recommended, as well as the many illuminative conversations we had, laid the foundation from which *handiwork* gradually rose. My thanks to Steve Wing, warden at the Cape Clear Bird Observatory, for his patience, wisdom and advice with regard to the bird-related aspects of my research, and to my landlady, whose generalised kindness and beautiful house have allowed me many hours of untroubled productivity. I must also acknowledge John Hutchinson, whose writings and teachings continue to influence me, perhaps most conspicuously here in this 'little book'. My enduring thanks to Lisa Coen, Sarah Davis-Goff, Laura Waddell and Lucy Luck for their magnanimous trust and unswerving diligence, and finally to Doireann Ní Ghríofa, Deborah Baume and Mark Beatty — my triumvirate — for their constancy, perspicacity, and care.